# A BRIGHTNESS TO CAST SHADOWS

Also by David Constantine

(editor and part-translator) *German Short Stories 2*, Penguin Parallel Texts (1976)

*The Significance of Locality in the Poetry of Friedrich Hölderlin* (MHRA, 1979)

# A BRIGHTNESS TO CAST SHADOWS

David Constantine

for Keith Turner
with my good wishes
David Constantine

BLOODAXE
BOOKS

ISBN: 0 906427 14 2 (ordinary edition)
0 906427 15 0 (signed edition of 25 numbered copies)

First published 1980 by
Bloodaxe Books
1 North Jesmond Avenue
Jesmond
Newcastle upon Tyne NE2 3JX

The publisher acknowledges the financial assistance
of Northern Arts

Printed in Great Britain by
Unwin Brothers Limited, Old Woking, Surrey

*For Helen*

## Acknowledgements

Acknowledgements are due to the editors of the following publications in which some of these poems have appeared: *Anglo-Welsh Review*, *Argo*, *New Poetry 5 and 6* (Hutchinson/Arts Council—P.E.N., 1979 and 1980), *Stand*, and *Workshop New Poetry*. Five poems selected from this collection also appear in the anthology *Ten North-East Poets* (Bloodaxe Books, 1980), together with a cycle of nine new poems not published here.

## Contents

## 'As our bloods separate'

As our bloods separate the clock resumes,
I hear the wind again as our hearts quieten.
We were a ring: the clock ticked round us
For that time and the wind was deflected.

The clock pecks everything to the bone.
The wind enters through the broken eyes
Of houses and through their wide mouths
And scatters the ashes from the hearth.

Sleep. Do not let go my hand.

## Birdsong

Most are sleeping, some
Have waited hopelessly for mercy,
Others even by this will not be stayed.
But we who have not slept for quantity
Of happiness have heard
The dawn precipitate in song
Like dewfall.

We think our common road a choir of trees.

## ‘Daffodils in vases’

Daffodils in vases, watch them daily
For the first touch of dying, even
The blossom you came carrying
Of cherry and almond I will raise
The fire with tonight to see
You naked by, only the tulips
Wider and wider leave them opening
Until their petals fall
In gouts on the marble hearth.

## 'But most you are like'

But most you are like
The helpless singing of birds
To whom the light happens
On whom it falls
And at whose purity of voice
The skies weep and there is a pause
In all the world before beginning
And before the ending.

## A Brightness to Cast Shadows

And now among them these dark mornings yours
Ascendant and of a brightness to cast shadows.
Love the winter, fear
The earlier and earlier coming of the light
When in the mantle blue we turn our dead faces.

## The Fool

Be still, only believe me, said the Fool
Love and with impartial pleasure
Touched her breasts and mine

Ignoring any history of lovers and children
But as a matter of sole beauty
Admired their present marks

On my breasts now and see, he said,
The lighter halo of hers. A while,
The dancers' above earth,

We did take hands she and I
And the Fool in a ring against
Outliving Time

Whom I saw sardonically looking
To enter the round between us
Facing the boy Love.

## The Damned

I see the damned are like this:
Loquacious to no effect, for ever
Coming to the end of their poor abilities,
Words failing them, neither

Their blows nor their embraces
Serving them better,
Incapable of nakedness
They rasp their hands on one another

Like two dead trees' branches
They sound the skull with a long finger,
Their speech is a sort of trepanning, lidless
The eyes watch barrenly for ever.

Dawn: slow fall of song . . . The sky
I imagine white, streaming with mercy.

## ‘All wraiths in Hell are single’

All wraiths in Hell are single though they keep
Company together and go in troops like sheep.
None meets a lover from the former world,
No souls go hand in hand, round each is curled
The river Acheron. They suffer most
Who violently joined the myriad host,
Who angrily to spite love in the face
Before their time intruded on that place,
Putting themselves by pride beyond recovery,
Beyond sight, beyond calling. They seem to be
Alive among the dead wishing the thing undone
By which they put themselves beyond Acheron.
Divested of anger, cold, without reprieve
*Sine die* along the riverbanks they grieve.
They hear one calling after love into the black
But cannot answer and cannot come back.

## 'Among those fortunate dwellers'

1

Among those fortunate dwellers on coasts and islands
  Someone had always seen her, on a morning
Of usual brightness, at his work. From point
  To point the bay was slung with surf and beyond
Among the combing waves she rode the warm dolphin.
  On coins and household pottery they made
Depictions of that favourite beast and dolphin-eyed
  Were the boats travelling her element.

2

The mountains were visible to navigators,
  Brief and tumultuous were the many streams,
Audible underground. Solitary in their work
  Herdsmen or hunters saw her. When from off their hearts
At dawn her cool long fingers slipped and like an edge
  Of surf she trailed her scalloped dress into
The daybreak, then they grieved, though they were kings, and set
  Her visitations down in elegy.

3

The seas are changed and every shore will disappoint us,
  Nor by the white sun nor the white full moon
On the whiteness of snow or the whiteness of limestone
  Shall we see her whom the ocean bore and who
Also loved mountains. We shall not discover even
  Shards or coins of her cities or papyri
But, like the moon stranded in daylight, there remain
  For us only the shells on sand and mountains.

4

Therefore admire her shell: the evidence of seas
   Between tides and between the deluges.
Admire the ribs convergent on a beak of land,
   The runnels in a delta; so the moon
Poured down on mound and combe and so the dawn they called
   The rosy-fingered opened on the sky.
From this, a coracle, she stepped and selvaged
   White and rose the surf withdrew behind her.

5

My fingers comb your delta of black hair, your fingers
   Rake my heart. From spring to rivermouth are not
All waters hers? The moorland at our backs
   Emptied the snow into the streams and raised
Like cicatrices were the many veins upon
   The body of the land and caged in ribs
The wild heart beat underground and we lay like the land
   Flooding, convergent on the estuaries.

## Streams

It was never enough only to trace their courses
Nor to follow alongside, and the best were pathless,
But I must be always in them straddling the waters,
Clawing among roots, fingers poked in the wet moss
And parting the long grasses for a grip of stone.
Best to be naked as well as possible to feel
The switch of birches, smooth trunks of rowan,
Sticks and fronds of fern and tassels of hazel.

Hand on either bank and foothold to embrace
The reclining falls and rainbowed round to sunder
The water like a tree for a breathless space . . .
And for the smell of mud there is in worming under
The grasses, the toppled boles are finger-soft
And the glimmering rock flakes like the bark of birches.
The eyes may be shut with moss in some such cleft,
Mouth and nose pressed to in a deep kiss.

One I remember climbing from the blue renowned
As deepest of all the lakes and verdant black
Among lawns and pines the enclosed garden ground
To where, between scented equal hills, my back
And praising arms brightly arrayed in sun,
Wet-lipped from a hoof of sedge the water grew.
You will have thought below I'd gone for heaven
When I stood there at the sky on the brink of all blue.

## 'In a dry season'

In a dry season
I have found the path they will have come
From their island of seven green fields
In the wine-dark waste
Housing behind walls.

The chimneys are stopped with nests,
The lintels have been unburdened;
But the thorns
Crouch from the wind still
That were set for shelter.

There out of a gateway
The path came walking on the moor
To the overhang of grey trees
Softened by moss among the gloaming boulders,
To the road low in the distance.

Aslant where they could
And otherwise by steps
And iron ladders:
A variety of ways to climb,
The best, but none easy.

By the roadside when
The stile steps down into ferns
And our drought has gone again under their waters
The building of a hard path to a home
In cloud would be remembered.

## The Drowned

Flat calm. The ships have gone.
By moonlight and by daylight one by one
Into a different world the drowned men rise
But cannot claw the sleep out of their eyes.
None such can know the bigger light from the less
Nor taste even the salt. Their heaviness
By no means may be leavened. Now they live
As timbers do where shipworms thrive
Only in what they feed. Strange things engross
The little galleries of thought after the loss
Of breath. The white clouds pass, but still
The drowned increase upon the senses till
The moon delivers them. On islands then
Seeing the lovely daylight watchful men
Come down and haul these burdens from the waves
And slowly cart them home and dig them graves.

## Lamb

A lamb lay under the thorn, the black
Thorn bending by the last broken wall
And grasping what it can.

The dead lamb picketed a ewe.
She cropped round, bleating
And chewing in that machinal way of sheep.
And although she backed to a safe distance,
When I climbed down towards her lamb
Through a gap in the wall,
It was as if painfully paying out the fastening cord.

The crow was there, also
At a safe distance, waiting for the ewe to finish;
And sidled off a further yard or so,
Waiting until I too should have finished.

In high relief the lamb
Lay leaping, the small hooves down-pointed at
The instant of spring, one foreleg already flexing
To step forward on the air.
The head like a new tennis ball,
But stained; the mouth grim as a shark's.
For the eye had gone, and all
That swelled from the socket was a black bubble.

The ewe, chewing and mourning, and
The crow, that fathoms the convenient eye-hole,
Had approached on either hand. The bubble burst
And a hole sank such a depth into the skull
That not a sound returned.

I backed away, and again
The ewe could circle the navel of her earth;
But the crow, with a hunching of wings and a jump sideways,
Glanced over the raised cloak of one wing,
And trod, and grasped its feet into the ground,
And could wait

Until hunger stretched and parted
The cord, and the monotony
Of chewing deadened any pain.

Even from river level I knew the place,
In the angle where the wall descends,
And I thought I could make out the bush,
And the white dot of the dead lamb under it.

And I thought in that place there is always an exit
From the light of the sun, an issue of darkness
Opened by the crow's black beak. I know the way,
Into the hillside,
Through the eye of a lamb.

That was in April, when
Snow still lies beyond the wall, before
The blackthorn flowers.

## Near Zennor

Coming among the grazing boulders
They herded them into hedges
And tended their own cattle on the vacated ground.

They made houses of the stones skirting the carn
And beyond mounds for their dead
In a quiet herd, and paths from place to place.

It is not easy now to distinguish between
Their circles and the collars of the dead mines.
The hedges and paths are as they were.

And a stone riven by frost from the mother flank
Their feet have gone over across water,
Their heads bowed under daily into the house.

To go back unobtrusively under the moor
Is one grace of austerity, to flower
And be quarried for a successor's building.

## The Lane

The lane's especial beauty, why especially
You are at home there, is the way it has
Of winding unhurriedly and for no remembered reason,
And this I have come to love more even than
The scent and the quiet between its hedges.

Even alone now, though by nature one
For landmarks on the horizon to be reached by dark,
As far as is possible I adopt your way
And walk in the lane's good time that never offers
More to our view than we should be content with;

And after the farm becomes impassable,
Under the vaulting of both hedges' trees,
In any season but of the hardest drought or frost:
Which ultimatum at the outset lends
Your dawdling its complacency.

For these your and the lane's own qualities
And that in special once, a moonless night
And close with honeysuckle,
The sea pausing between wave and wave,
You came to meet me down it,

Nowhere is more home. A certainty
Of love is that of taking hands
And elsewhere turning into this same lane,
Sending ahead the old precursors:
The fox, the cat, the finches.

## Journey

Leaving the watered villages
The ash and poplar·cool in their appearances
We came the companionable stream and I
To the last farm by and by.

For the whitethorn there
That was in flower later than anywhere
The girl water would not continue with me
I left her under the last tree.

Then some days following
I cast the long shadows of morning and evening
At noon I rode the sun on my shoulder
I was without water.

The white sheep lay
Like the remaining snow in February
On the north side of walls, in holes they hid
In poor embraces of shade.

Beyond pasture, beyond enclosure
On the common land of rock how far below were
Any cwm, any cradled pool and the water-veined
Wide folds. There intervened

No cloud, no bough between
Myself and the sun, only a hawk was shone
Steadily upon me in the grip of noon
I trod my shadow down.

I dreamed of the girl Artemis
She wore the ash and the poplar in a green dress
She led three burning hounds and seeing me
She smiled and set them free.

## 'Pitiless wind'

Pitiless wind, the hedges
Queue for dole, there is
No warmth in line. More
Pitiless light, searching
From under snowclouds, level

Like the wind, discovering
Rags, cans and what
Have been hugged to the heart
Since May: nests, all
Empty but one or two

And these, harboured since there
Were leaves, containing small
Frail skeletons bent
Like embryos. The wind, the light
Show up our few belongings.

## 'The wind has bared the stars'

The wind has bared the stars,
The skeletons, the after-images.

The life of trees has flown,
Their swarm of leaves, their hail of birds, their bone-

Dry sticks tap-tap,
Their blades slant in the earth's cold lap,

And leafless we are shown
To be rooted apart, two trees not one.

The dust and hail belong
Nowhere particular, our leaves and song;

Disperse among the stars,
Our skeletons, our after-images.

## "Trewernick"

1

House in the marsh, it was always at evening
   We saw you first, over reed-tops, through a haze
Of lichened willows, after twelve hours travelling.
   Beyond our terminus the daylight set
Slowly from off the remaining terra firma,
   But we retraced our passage through the reeds
To the gate and threshold among apple trees before
   The night came roosting in your cypresses.
House in the marsh, had you taught your children nothing
   But the reliable grace of such a welcome
Yet you had charged a family for generations
   So that they shone with the warm glow of gold.

2

Mounding the earth, facing it in with rusty stone,
   Raising upon the borders of culture
Fine distinctions in heather and broom gently you made
   Your garden join the field, your tended plants
Confused their colours with a savage hedge behind
   Of gorse and bramble. Had I to indicate
Your tact with rooted lives I'd put my finger on
   That sewing of your garden to the fields
Which rise then stitched with hedges in a mild gradient
   To Ludgvan Church and culminate on ground
Of granite where the brow is wreathed with defences
   And the threadbare back pockmarked with tumuli.

3

One year the marvel was a bush vermilion
With lucent fruit, one bush, glowing like Mars,
Kept at its brilliant prime for us to see. There followed
By our hands the abundant bleeding of the tree,
The million berries mounded in a basket. Your
Own skill is that of transferring the garden
Into the recesses of the house, of cupping
The summer in a household hoard with no
Diminishing of warmth or light. In jars on shelves
In cupboards stood the store of amber, garnet,
Jade and when the year closed down the house glowed at its core
With the essences your working hands put by.

4

Dear ones in Cornwall how golden and leisurely
The light stays. Nobody can be in haste
Not even to ask for or dispose of stories,
But a shyness which is perhaps the sun
Slanting so low causes companions to hide their eyes
And soonest to fall silent, admiring
The growth of a tree set at a birth ten years ago.
Then to seek anything would seem discourteous
In the fullness we can almost hold to be lasting.
Again we shall leave and you will write to us
How in October the sky blackened with starlings
And fell on that mock cornfield like a pall.

5

But now the children are handing you down apples
  That will sweeten the dark under the roof
Another winter. Then the reeds, under a cold sky,
  Are warm-coloured like corn and fire by fire
Towards another spring you burn the logs of cypress
  And apple wood. How much is into us
Of all your gifts and through the long attenuation
  Shall we be able to keep hold? Think the hands
We see on tombs are clasped not only in farewell
  But to impart and thereby are we bound.
By touch the generations glow. If not reunion
  Those held hands are at least continuance.

## 'Suddenly she is radiant again'

Suddenly she is radiant again.
She sees rainbows through her wet lashes;
In the brilliant light her wet cheeks glisten;
Her talk resumes like a brook, as fast and careless.

She has to suffer the interruption
Of sobs still, that have the bad manners
To arrive after the thunder has already gone
Over the hill, insisting they are hers.

We were a black sky only a minute ago,
Now I'm the one cloud in her clear heaven.
I haven't even begun yet to undo
The hideous knot of anger she tied me in.

I'm like a black old lump of winter snow
Bitterly facing the spring sun. Fair
Is always fair and the ugly, be they ever so
Much in the right, are not welcome anywhere.

I'm not a stone, I'm dirty snow that in
Her sunlight melts. It has no choice but to.
Soon I begin to feel I've been forgiven:
I go down on my knees and fasten her shoe.

## 'For years now'

For years now through your face the skull has shown
Nearer than through their living surface
The hills' bulk of dead stone;

And for years, watching you sleeping in that chair,
I have wished you might die with your face and hands composed,
Quietly sleeping there,

And trusted death to be so easy on you
That now one moment you would be sleeping and now
Have ceased without seeming to.

But today, watching you dead, I cannot think that there
Is any such slow passing into death from life
That the one might seem the other.

Finally the gap is absolute. Living
At all you were never nearly dead
And dead there is nothing

Vital of you in the abandoned face.
But the lack, the difference, has such nearness
We could almost embrace.

## Waiting

We have gathered together
The things you will need immediately
And set them on a table
By the bed you will be born in.
You have three drawers to your name
Of clothes for the first months.

I go from room to room. The house
Is waiting. Our hands are ready.
Even not yet knowing you
We love you; grateful
For how you have increased us; glad
We have it in us to put out new love.

## Hands

Round my finger, like a bird perching . . .
In my hollow palm, like a pebble, a cool bud . . .
Idling with his hands.

O hands . . .

The interslotting of our fingers and beckoning in
Your palm and tonguing of
The skin that tautens between thumb and index . . .
Your hand gives him the breast and the ring shines.

How cold her hands were latterly, and visible
The painful jointings of the long bones.
The firelight shone almost through and the blood's
Network with its many nodes and bruises
Was shown like that of a leaf.
She lagged her ring with cotton but
The days loosened it again.

His sharp nails are like
The fragments of rosy shell lying in pools.

O sands, o future rocks . . .

## In Memoriam 8571 Private J.W. Gleave

who was at Montauban, Trônes Wood and Guillemont

*'So many without memento . . .'* (In Parenthesis)

1. *Prologue: The Children*

I bade them climb: they must have come to the very crest
And it was beautiful to see them shine
Not steadily but charged at a sudden moment
And for only such duration as the light allowed
The light they caught upon their faces from the face
Already we should have thought sunk out of sight.

There are some dead we see and even see by;
They glimmer for a generation, our looking
Lends them more luminance. I saw the father,
Whom no-one can rekindle, appear to shine
Over the earth in the eyes of the gazing children.
They cast his face upon my white paper.

2. *After how many Novembers . . .*

How soon, I wonder, after how many Novembers
  Did the years begin to seem not paces
Interminably around a pit nor steps deserting
  A place, but slow degrees by which she came
Over the curve of the world into that hemisphere
  His face rose in? Again we have given ground,
The dark advances an hour into the afternoon,
  In the interlude between cloud and horizon
A mild sun scythes the field—so by the last winter
  After an illness and before her death
We saw a similar light dawn on the woman
  Who had been a widow more than fifty years.

She lingered in the doorway of the living-room
  Impelled as people leaving are to say
Some word more than goodnight. I have seen her eyes shining
  Bright as a young girl's on that threshold
Bright with tears. She found nothing to say. But having
  Her purse in hand—the purse she had kept house from
For generations since the Queen died—she took out
  The new, neat, folded notes of her pension
And to the children and their children and their child
  Disposed of these. We do not like to watch
A person look for words nor by whatever gestures
  Taking her leave of table, hearth and chair.

She went to her own room where everything was ready
  To leave, the furniture of her married life
Though in another house, one he had never seen.
  But in that mirror he had seen his face,
They will have stood side by side and looked at themselves
  She will have stood by herself and remembered.
And always she held the two or three photographs
  Which light had fallen on man and wife to make
In an envelope with the notice of his death
  As if to cross over with these in hand
That she should know him again who had been effaced
  And he should know her who had lived and aged.

3. *Notification*

It was the painful duty of Lieutenant Thomas Dinsdale
On Army Form B 104-82
In an envelope the postwoman shrank from touching
To notify my grandmother of her altered state.
The women stood by, they followed the post like crows:
To whom would such a communication come
That morning, to what woman by the hand of a woman
Whose job it was daily to visit that village of streets
And lay the stigmata on certain doors?

So the news came from Guillemont to Salford 5
After a lapse of weeks during which time
She had known no better than to believe herself a wife.

### 4. *By word of mouth*

Not having seen him die and when
Upon their notification nothing followed
Neither the body to her hearth
Nor any of the late soldier's effects
A little while
As though the outcome could be put in doubt
She trimmed her mourning with a thread of hope
She kept the Suitor from her husband's chair
Showed Death the door
Nightly, until the evenings were long.
He called then with a companion from France.
The neighbours, who miss nothing, saw
Only the soldier leave.

### 5. *Rêcit*

No messenger in the tragedies
So mean but coming to the wife, the mother
Or any beloved woman waiting
Recounts fittingly the dead man's death
In alexandrines or iambics
And honours him in the telling.
But who the pal was is not remembered
Nor what he said, nor what the questions were
She had the heart to put nor whether
She lamented there and then, praising the qualities
Of the man lost and hiding her face as queens do
In her apron. Not a word, not the place itself
Reached me in his pronunciation
But as to how and where

She only shrugged her shoulders
And perhaps she had that from the messenger
Who did not tell her that the night was very short
And began in a barrage of phosgene gas
And ended in a thick fog
And a barrage of high explosive
As they moved around the southern edge of Trônes Wood
Across seven hundred yards of open ground
Gently sloping to the village of Guillemont
In an attack understood to be hopeless
But serving the French on their right
Whose attack was also hopeless
And that somewhere before the wire
He was obliterated
In gas and night and fog.

6.

But by November the congregation of widows
  Being told it was a reasonable sacrifice
Their men had made saw mutilated trees bedecked
  With bloody tatters and being nonetheless
Promised a resurrection of the body
  They saw God making their men anew out of
The very clay. These women having heard from soldiers
  However little from the battlefield
Towards All Saints gathered black gouts from the elder
  Among their children stared at the holy tree
And envied Christ his hurts fit to appear in.
  Some then insisted on a photograph
Taken before the harm was done—which face they caused
  To appear in the hideous crater of their lives
Upon its slimy water. In time while she pursued
  With wrung hands her business as a widow
The water cleared. On the surface of a peaceful pool
  Decently framed the face shone steadily.

7.

There being no grave, there being not even one
Ranked among millions somewhere in France,
Her grief went without where to lay its head.
She would have rested sooner had she had
Or had she even learned somewhere there was
A well-kept place where he was lying dead.

She could not even think him out of harm:
He must be hurt somewhere by every shell,
Somewhere his mouth could not get breath for gas.
She would have scavenged all his body home
Into the shelter of if not her house
At least the roofed and hidden well-walled grave.

But of what comfort is the body home
Which here or there cannot embrace or smile?
And of what comfort is the body whole?
Only the rich and saints do not corrupt.
She almost thought there were degrees of death
And he was more dead piecemeal and abroad.

There being nowhere but the family grave
She went and called her grief out of the air
And coaxed it to alight upon the stone
That did not bear his name. Upon that absence
She grieved as though it were the greater one
And death was lured almost within her view.

She set that feature on the featureless
Visibly everlasting plain of death
She trod a path, she made some little inroad
And placing three or four remembrance days
She netted in their few interstices
Glimpses that she could bear out of the deep.

8. *Roll of Honour*

She never saw his name at Thiepval
Nor even in Manchester Cathedral
But on Liverpool Street outside the Mission Hall
There was a Roll of Honour on the wall

Affixed in nineteen-seventeen
And this she will have seen
Daily (until the Blitz
Blew all the names to bits).

The enlisted men—there were no officers—
Were columned street by street and hers
Was one of those already crossed. By rights
The Vicar should have come at nights

And crossed the others one by one
Until the toll was done.

9. *Like shrapnel*

Like shrapnel in the lucky ones
She carried fragments in her speech
Remarkable to grandchildren
But to herself accustomed
Like rise and shine and left
Left . . . he had a good home and he left
And a long, long trail a-winding . . .

## Coltsfoot

Coming before my birthday they are forever your flowers
Who are dead and at whose hand
I picked them on the allotments and blitzed land.

## Coltsfoot and Larches

I love coltsfoot that they
Make their appearance into life among dead grass:
Larches, that they
Die colourfully among sombre immortals.

## Hyacinth

Overnight the hyacinth opened
In the room left to itself among
Our books and pictures, behind
The closed door and the drawn curtains
Where the chairs had sat the fire out.

By morning the door opened strangely.
The scent glowed through the flower's long fingers
The hand turned for my praise, and as between
Mirrors I saw your face in that dark room
Receding down the years of familiar rooms.

Though windows gleamed and the sky rose
And the ground was already prickly with shoots
Still the unthinking birds whom we can think
Undying, the jackdaw, the white gull,
Called from our roof: 'Remember! Remember!'

Everything reminds. Though into such rose dawns
The roads take up their travellers
And run with a straight intent
Or climb purposefully to ridges
Having such skies behind

Still throughout today and for
Its time consuming in our element
The rose hyacinth has burned
And I have watched faces returning
Down a flight of rooms for want of light.

## Patience and Labour

Patience: or
I should expect nothing; but
Of patience I will expect nothing;

Nor of labour, also
A requirement, and
I will labour,

Without hope in either
Patience or labour, for both
Are within my power.

## Johnny

Faces, faces, says Johnny,
The perceptions lingering, lingering, in general
And in the home, for what
Does a man see on the dead wall of his life,
A jakes wall, but among the writing
Faces, faces, beating the brow against?

## Jimmy

The belly: a big craw
Come out of the shirt like a goitre;
An angry cross of scars.

Jimmy, your face has the texture of fungus.
Your tears drop like fat
In rapid beads, from under the hair
The head is weeping,

They hit the table between your bloody knuckles.

## Billy

The lines, Billy, I am thinking
I should like to run a finger down, they rive
Your face to the bone chin.

Your daughter, you are saying, said
The aborted one, Norma, 15, fuck off
Back to the asylum Dad, your own dad,
You are saying, home
From prison strung you to the mangle naked
And beat you to a jelly. I

Am thinking Billy when he weeps
It is the rent, the creases fill but
What about the rent? And more
Than ever I should like to put a finger in
The runnels of your face
That wants some beating for cadaverousness.

## Stuart

Stuart, I would not begin at once
With the obvious. It seems
Too many have and she
Is none the warmer. Her beak
Would gnaw through bone.

The mouth, I grant you, is
A whiskerless rat's; raw
Her hands and one of those trees on the estate
The kids have stripped
Would be as abundant to embrace.

Under hers, as motherly as hail,
The child has lost his tongue. Where then
Should you begin? The eyes
Look for the worst. Could you only
Show them some goodwill.

## 'But with a history of ECT'

But with a history of ECT
And separation Milburn Margaret Mrs
Did not attain the obliterating sea
She got no further than the DHSS
And on a Friday in the public view
Lodged on the weir as logs do.

During the rush-hour she was attended to
And all the terraces of Gallowgate
Watched the recovery of this female who
Went in the river at the age of thirty-eight.
She did not pass unnoticed but instead
Got seen to being dead.

And at the inquest the Acting Coroner
Inquiring as to how and why she died
Exculpated both the hospital and her
Emeritus husband who identified
That frozen woman in the mortuary
He had four children by.

## ‘Dennis Jubb is dead’

Dennis Jubb is dead. But considering
He certainly never went short of smokes
Nor a dreg of something in the morning
Not to mention the lovely picture books

He often sat behind his barrow in doorways
Grinning at the innocent passers-by over
And when you take into account that all these
Were extras to a living wage we do aver

That Mr Dennis Jubb did not do too bad
Bearing in mind as well all the other things he had
As for example he had a loving mate
And a revitalized house on the Fairhope Road Estate

And that he lived to be forty, a good age,
And got his death by burning on the front page.

## ‘I suppose you know this isn’t a merry-go-round’

I suppose you know this isn’t a merry-go-round.
The man won’t stop it when you think you’ve had your money’s worth.
To get off at all you’ll have to jump
And risk breaking your neck
And where you fall will appear strange
And not where you got on.

These have not been flat revolutions
On the enduring earth
But spirals down.
You are lower now.

That being so
I would almost advise you to stay put.
You are in the company of your friends
And for a change
You can always stagger from a horse to a white elephant.
Nobody seems to mind.

**David Constantine** was born in 1944 in Salford, Lancashire. He read Modern Languages at Wadham College, Oxford, where he wrote a doctoral thesis on the poetry of Hölderlin and taught himself Greek. Since 1969 he has been a lecturer in German at Durham University; he is married, with two children. His poems and short stories have been published in various magazines and anthologies. A selection appears in the anthology *Ten North-East Poets* (Bloodaxe Books, 1980); *A Brightness to Cast Shadows* is his first collection of poems.

**Arthur Byrne** was born in 1949 in Davyhulme, near Manchester. After studying at Manchester College of Art & Design and Sheffield Polytechnic School of Art & Design, he helped found the Charlotte Press Printmaking Workshop in Newcastle and ran its etching department. Now a self-employed artist, he has shown paintings and prints in nine one-man exhibitions and at many group shows. The front cover shows 'Rhododendrons 7', one of a series of oil paintings. Studio address: 41 Edward Street, Pickering Nook, Burnopfield, Newcastle upon Tyne NE16 6EP.